FOOTBALL
PUZZLES

FOOTBALL PUZZLES

Sandy Ransford

**Illustrated by
David Mostyn**

MACMILLAN CHILDREN'S BOOKS

First published 1998 by
Macmillan Children's Books
a division of Macmillan Publishers Ltd
25 Eccleston Place, London SW1W 9NF
and Basingstoke

Associated companies throughout the world

ISBN 0 330 35409 4

1 3 5 7 9 8 6 4 2

A CIP catalogue record for this book is available from the British Library.

Printed and bound in Great Britain by
Mackays of Chatham plc, Chatham, Kent.

Contents

Rules of the Game

1 How many players are there in a soccer team?

2 Who in the team can handle the ball?

3 With which parts of their bodies may players move the ball?

4 How many linesmen are there?

5 How do the linesmen signal to the referee?

6 How many substitutes are allowed in a game of football?

7 How long is each half of play?

8 How long is the half-time interval?

9 What does the ball have to do for a goal to be scored?

10 If the ball stops on the touchline, is it out of play?

11 What is an indirect free kick?

12 If a player takes a corner kick, how far away from him must his opponent be?

13 How much should a football weigh?

14 What must a goalkeeper wear?

15 Can the ball be changed during the game?

Afternoon Out

It's Saturday afternoon and you're off to the match. But how good are you at working out what your money will buy?

1   If your bus fare is 80p each way, and it costs £10 to get into the ground, and you spend 50p on a drink when you're there, how many 2p sweets can you buy on the way home if you started out with £13?

2   If the ground holds 50,000 people, and it is 65 per cent full, how many people are at the match?

3   If, on your way home, you decide you don't want any sweets, but, together with your friend, you'd like some fish and chips, how much money would you have to borrow from your friend if a portion of fish is £1.20 and a portion of chips is 85p?

Woolly Mufflers

How many football scarves can you spot in the picture?

Picture Puzzle

This crossword has both picture and word clues, so you should find it easy to solve.

Across

 1 There are two at the goal (4)
 5 Game (5)
 6 A _ _ _ _ _ _ kick is taken from the quarter circle by the flag (6)
 7 All 11 players (4)
 9 He might be a right or a left (4)
10 *Picture Clue* (3)
12 *Picture Clue* (4)
14 What you do with the ball (4)
16 *Picture Clue* (10)
18 *Picture Clue* (7)
21 *Picture Clue* (4)
22 Queen's _ _ _ _ Rangers (4)
23 Association football (6)
24 *Picture Clue* (7)

Down

 2 *Picture Clue* (5)
 3 *Picture Clue* (4)
 4 It's behind the goal line (9)
 7 Intercept player with ball (6)
 8 A penalty kick is taken from the penalty _ _ _ _ (4)
11 *Picture Clue* (4)
13 Another name for a mid-fielder (4-3)
15 *Picture Clue* (8)
16 The aim of the game (4)
17 Another name for a forward (7)
19 *Picture Clue* (6)
20 *Picture Clue* (5)

First Half

How many differences can you spot between these two scenes of a match?

Name-dropping

Listed below are the names of some very well-known players of past and present, both British and international, but the letters have been jumbled up. Can you work out who they are?

1 JEVION NINES

2 COAL LED RAT RIM

3 NINK JAMS GLEN RUN

4 THROB BABY CLON

5 PAPER JAR PINE IN E

6 GONE MAID ADORA

7 COUG PAGES NAIL

8 LADY G HEN SLINK

9 CAFF JONY HUR

10 GRAB BORE, GI TOO

11 TONI CAN RACE

12 NK RILEY RAGE

Cup Tie

Which of these pictures of the FA Cup is the mirror image of the top left-hand one?

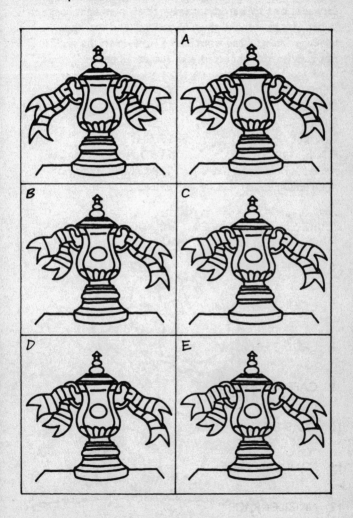

Free Kick

Find all the words listed below in the grid opposite. The words may read across, up, down or diagonally, either forwards or backwards, but they are all in straight lines. When you have found them all you will find that the left-over letters, read from left to right down the grid, spell out two words connected with successful teams.

CENTRE LINE (2 lines)

COACH

DIVING

DRIBBLE

FOUL

KICK OFF (2 lines)

MIDFIELD

OFFSIDE

OWN GOAL (2 lines)

PASS

PITCH

STUD

THROW IN (2 lines)

WING

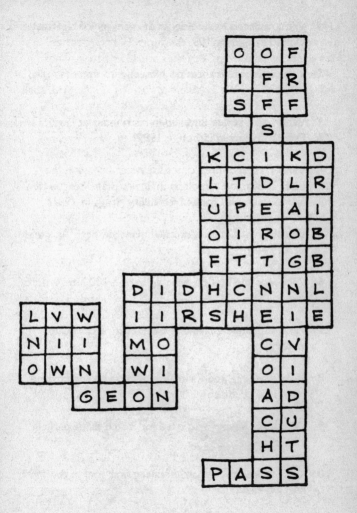

Who?

1 Who replaced Kevin Keegan as manager of Newcastle United in January 1997?

2 Who is Edson Arantes do Nascimento better known as?

3 Who had a statue unveiled in his honour at Benfica's Estadio da Luz in Lisbon in 1992?

4 Who was sold three times for record sums in the early 1980s, led Napoli to their first Italia League title in 1987 and was banned for taking drugs in 1991?

5 Which great Dutch footballer managed both Ajax and Barcelona?

6 Who was the first Englishman to win 100 international caps?

7 Who captained England in their 1966 World Cup victory?

8 Who was knighted for managing the winning England team in that match?

9 Which goalkeeper was tried for match-fixing early in 1997?

10 Who scored the record-breaking first goal in the 1997 FA Cup Final?

On the Line

Do you know what these linesman's signals mean?

Odd One Out

Circle the odd one out in each of these series of words.

1 Ibrox, Bramall Lane, Hampden Park.

2 Front block, side block, trapping.

3 Juventus, Spartak, Dynamo.

4 Santos, Nacional, Sao Paulo.

5 Link-man, winger, centre striker.

6 Volley, chip, dribble.

7 Out-swinger, underarm throw, long throw.

8 Heading, tripping, obstruction.

9 Centre forward, forward short leg, inside forward.

10 Rose Bowl, UEFA Cup, World Cup.

Knotty Problem

Which laces belong to which boot?

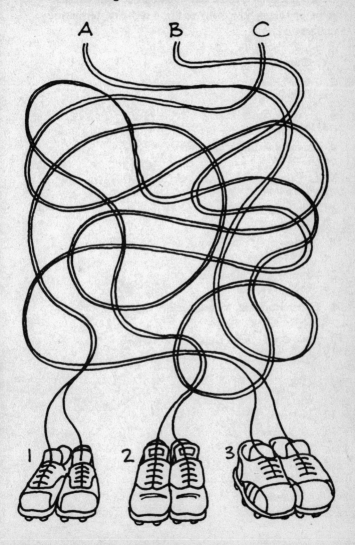

What's in a Name?

Check how much you really know about your favourite game by seeing how many of these technical terms you understand.

1 Offside.

2 Free kick.

3 Foul.

4 Penalty.

5 Throw-in.

6 Yellow card.

7 Red card.

8 Flick pass.

9 Bending.

10 Half volley.

11 Diving.

12 Punching.

What's Missing?

Each of these pictures lacks one detail present in the top left-hand one. Can you spot what it is in each drawing?

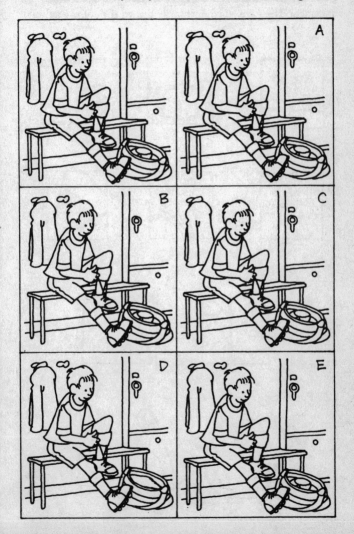

Gridlock

Each of the enlarged squares below matches exactly one of the squares in the picture opposite. Can you spot which they are? They are not necessarily drawn the right way up!

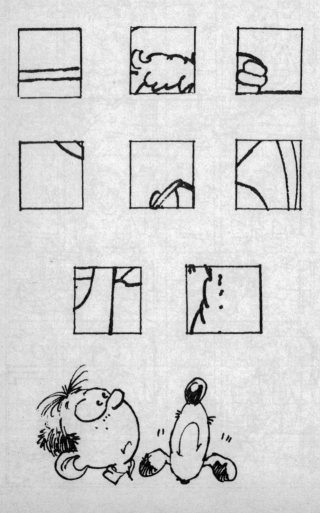

Getting Fit

Solve the clues and enter the answers in the grid. If you solve them correctly you will find, reading down the arrowed column, the name of one of Britain's most exciting young footballers.

1 These exercises are hard work on the arm muscles. (5-3)

2 You might do this on a bike or upside down in the air. (7)

3 If you do too many exercises you might end up like this! (9)

4 You need to do a lot of this up and down the field when playing football. (7)

5 This is a slower version of number 4. (7)

6 All the answers in this puzzle might come under this heading. (8)

7 Propelling yourself through water. (8)

8 Your keep-fit routines need to be this. (7)

9 Keeping fit consists of doing lots of these. (9)

Field of Play

Can you name these players' positions?

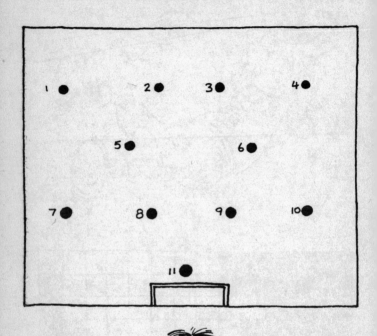

Fill the Gaps

Every other letter is missing from these teams' names. Can you work out what they are? (NB They're all British clubs.)

1 _ E _ D _ _ N _ T _ D

2 _ I _ B _ E _ O _

3 _ H _ R _ T _ N _ T _ L _ T _ C

4 _ H _ L _ E _ _

5 _ A _ C _ E _ T _ R _ N _ T _ D

6 _ O _ T _ N _ A _ _ O _ S _ U _

7 _ S _ O _ _ I _ L _

8 _ R _ S _ O _ _ O _ E _ S

9 _ R _ S _ O _ _ O _ T _ _ N _

10 _ A _ T _ C _ _ H _ S _ L _

11 _ E _ B _ _ O _ N _ Y

12 _ O _ V _ R _ A _ P _ O _ _ A _ D _ R _ R _

Odd Picture Out

Which of these six pictures is different from all the others, and why?

Make It Fit

This is a kind of clueless crossword. All you have to do is fit the words below into the grid opposite. Two letters have been given to help you – which should be all you need!

4-letter words
AREA
HALF
TIME
TRIP

5-letter words
BLOCK
BLUES
COACH
EXTRA
FIRST
SCORE
SCOUT
SPEED
SWIFT
UNFIT

6-letter words
ATTACK
LEAGUE

7-letter words
BRITAIN
CAPTAIN
CAUTION
SWEEPER
WINNING

8-letter words
DIVISION
OUTFIELD
TRAINING

9-letter word
TURNSTILE

12-letter word
HANDKERCHIEF

Nicknames

Do you recognize these British teams from their nicknames?

1 Minster Men

2 Blades

3 Villans

4 Hammers

5 Pensioners/Blues

6 Potters

7 Gunners

8 Swans

9 Rams

10 Irons

11 Biscuit Men

12 The Bhoys

13 Terrors

14 Lions

15 Stags

How Many?

How many different patterns are there on these footballs?

Word Snake

All the foreign teams listed below can be found in the grid opposite, in the order given. The words form a continuous line, reading up, down, right or left but *not* diagonally. Every letter in the grid is used once only.

AJAX AMSTERDAM

ANDERLECHT

BAYERN MUNICH

BENFICA

BOCA JUNIORS

FEYENOORD

FK AUSTRIA

FLAMENGO

INTERNAZIONALE

MILLONARIOS

PENAROL

REAL MADRID

SPARTA PRAGUE

VASCO DA GAMA

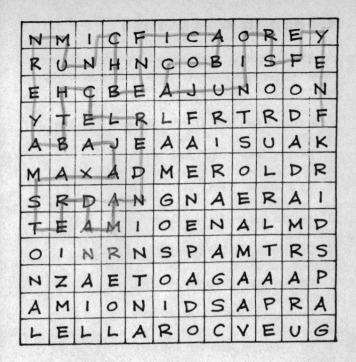

Hidden in a Sentence

A number of 'football' words are hidden in the sentences below. Can you spot them all? Here's an example to help you.

'Is that **man a Ger**man?' (The hidden word is 'manager'.)

1. 'Does he wear a cap, T.A., in winter?'

2. 'It's a wide fen, Cecil.'

3. 'Are the soldiers for war, Daniel?'

4. 'Did you show Fifi El Dorado?'

5. 'Lift him under the armpit, Charles.'

6. 'Don't scoff, Sid Edwards.'

7. 'Have you met Tessa Vernon?'

8. 'Show Caleb all the pictures, Harry.'

9. 'I'm not late, am I?'

10. 'Is that a corn, Errol?'

Striking

Which of the strikers pictured below is the one shown above in silhouette?

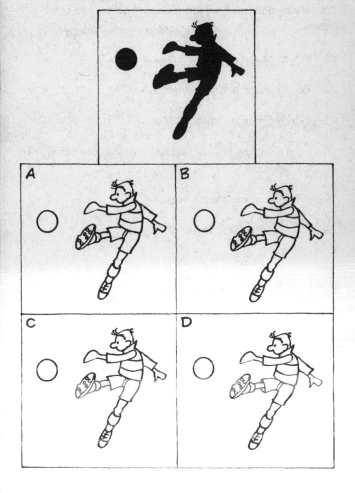

Observation Test

How good are your powers of observation? Test them by looking carefully at the picture opposite for just half a minute (time yourself with a watch), covering it up and then seeing how many of the questions below you can answer.

1 Which player is doing press-ups?

2 Which player is lifting weights?

3 Which player is skipping?

4 How many players are playing football in the corner of the field?

5 What are these players wearing?

6 What is the coach wearing?

7 In which hand is his whistle?

8 How many trees are there in the background?

9 What can you see over the hedge?

10 How many players are running round the field?

11 Who is wearing a woolly scarf round his neck?

Results and Records

1 Who holds the record for being both the youngest British international player and the youngest scorer in an FA Cup Final?

2 Who, in 1993, was FIFA World Footballer of the Year and named Footballer of the Year by both *World Soccer Magazine* and a French football magazine?

3 What is the record number of goals scored by one player in a World Cup Final?

4 Which team has won the FA Cup the greatest number of times?

5 What's the highest transfer fee ever paid for a player?

6 Which British player made the most international appearances?

7 What's the world record number of goals scored by one player in one game?

8 Who was the first British player to win the Golden Boot award as Europe's leading scorer?

9 Who has won the Scottish League Cup the greatest number of times?

10 Who has won the Football League Cup five times?

11 Who holds the world record for international goal-scoring by an England player?

Header!

How many differences can you spot between these two pictures of a great header?

Buying Kit

Rich, kind Uncle Henry has given you £100 for your birthday, which you want to spend on the strip of your favourite club. You'd also like a new pair of boots, a pair of socks, and a new football. When you arrive at the shop, you find everything is very expensive, and the boots and football come in a wide range of prices. How can you buy the best you can afford and still have £10 over to spend on a favourite video?

£16.99

£29.99

a. £19.99 b. £23.99
c. £29.99

£6.99

a. £9.99 b. £12.99
c. £15.99 d. £19.99

Rhyme Time

Match the pictures below with the words with which they rhyme.

**BOUGHT   PITCH   CATCH   NOTCH
BRISTLE   GATE   SOCKS**

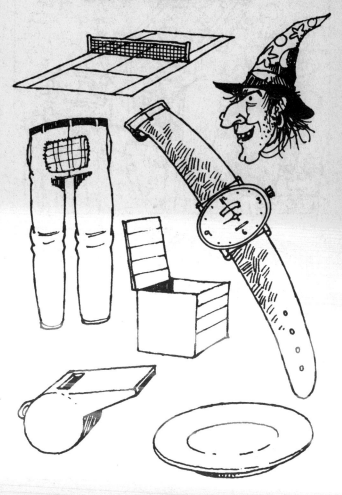

Own Goal!

Which two pictures of this unfortunate footballer are exactly the same?

41

Home Grounds

Match the teams on the left with their home grounds on the right.

1	Manchester United	St Andrews
2	Juventus	Molineux
3	Arsenal	Anfield Road
4	Barcelona	Loftus Road
5	Marseille	Stamford Bridge
6	Liverpool	Old Trafford
7	Rangers	Highbury
8	Everton	Hillsborough
9	Wolverhampton Wanderers	Delle Alpi
10	Stirling Albion	Vélodrome
11	Chelsea	Ibrox Park
12	Coventry City	Non Camp
13	Birmingham City	Goodison Park
14	Queen's Park Rangers	Annfield Park
15	Sheffield Wednesday	Highfield Road

Cup Fever

Do you recognize these famous football trophies?

1.

2.

3.

4.

Pitching In

How much do you know about the pitch on which you play your favourite game?

1 What's the diameter of the centre circle?

2 What's the minimum height of the corner flag above the ground?

3 What are the dimensions of the goal?

4 Are goalposts square or round in section?

5 What's the name of this rectangle?

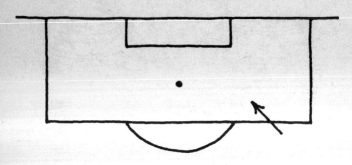

6 Can a soccer field be more than 130 yards long?

Team Badges 1

Can you identify these six British team badges?

1.

2.

3.

4.

5.

6.

Cryptic Crossword

This puzzle is strictly for crossword addicts, as it has a number of cryptic clues, just like an adult crossword. The key is to work them out bit by bit.

Across

1 Twelve inches, Queen Elizabeth – gives slang name for your favourite sport (6)
4 Ten and one gives a team (6)
7 Al gets left – and everyone (3)
8 United Nations keeps things in order – disorderly (6)
10 Northern British city ends with sandwich filling (6)
12 South, north or tea, initially, makes a horse noise (5)
15 Ajax Amsterdam player is this (5)
17 He or she has possession (5)
19 Belonging to Roman X, frequently (5)
20 Restore – regarding something just made (5)
22 Speak quietly without mother at the beginning – also means speak (5)
25 Scottish rap gives a small piece (5)
28 Speedy, east, north – do up buttons (6)
29 Hit with top part of body – into net? (6)
30 Number one card – very clever! (3)
31 Famous Parisian tower (6)
32 Change direction (6)

Down

1 Dirtied – or played on fairly (6)
3 Sun's beam, on – gives a kind of fabric (5)
4 Kind of tree is older (5)
6 Six is one, so is one (6)
9 Person who sells tickets – often at high prices (4)
11 It may be sung in church or at a match (4)
12 Demonstrates (5)
13 Not inner (5)

46

14 Heavy weight above – describes someone who rides a motorbike at over 100 mph (3-2)

16 America, east, means employ (3)

18 Keep it on the ball! (3)

20 Type of ticket you buy hoping to win something (6)

21 Goals have them, fish avoid them (4)

23 Scored equally (4)

24 Conundrum (see next page?) (6)

26 Can Al sail a boat on it? (5)

27 Gives pain (your legs may do this after too much football!) (5)

Riddle-me-ree

Solve the riddle.

My first is in tackle but never in shoot,
My second's in dribble but never in boot.
My third is in volley and also in view,
My fourth's in the centre of ref and of new.
My fifth is in Rangers and also Montrose,
My sixth is in practice, professional and prose.
My seventh whole letter is round, like a ball,
My eighth is the same, as wide as it's tall.
My ninth's in pullover, but never in jersey,
My whole is a team that plays on the Mersey.

Right and Left

How many right and how many left football boots can you spot in the picture? Note that the stripes are on the outside of the boots.

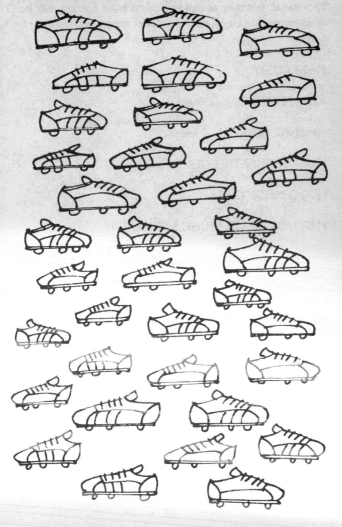

Great Names

The names of all the famous coaches and managers listed below can be found in the grid. The words may read across, up, down or diagonally, either forwards or backwards, but they are all in straight lines. Letters may be used more than once, but not all the letters are necessarily used.

MATT BUSBY

ALEX FERGUSON (2 lines)

HELENIO HERRERA (2 lines)

JOSEF 'SEPP' HERBERGER (3 lines)

HUGO MEISL (2 lines)

MARINUS 'RINUS' MICHELS (2 lines)

FERENC PUSKAS (2 lines)

ALF RAMSEY (2 lines)

TELE SANTANA (2 lines)

HELMUT SCHON (2 lines)

GUSZTAV SEBES (2 lines)

BILL SHANKLY (2 lines)

GIOVANNI TRAPATTONI (2 lines)

M	A	T	T	B	U	S	B	Y	N	M	F	G
I	A	T	L	S	I	E	M	L	P	R	E	O
C	N	R	L	S	K	B	T	K	R	E	R	I
H	H	G	I	N	Q	E	L	N	A	G	G	N
E	E	U	B	N	L	S	C	A	M	R	U	E
L	R	S	G	E	U	N	N	H	S	E	S	L
S	R	Z	I	O	D	S	E	S	E	B	O	E
A	E	T	O	F	M	E	R	D	Y	R	N	H
K	R	A	V	E	K	P	E	I	L	E	O	E
S	A	V	A	S	Q	P	F	G	N	H	H	L
U	B	L	N	O	B	D	L	V	W	U	C	M
P	E	J	N	J	A	N	A	T	N	A	S	U
X	W	N	I	N	O	T	T	A	P	A	R	T

What's Wrong?

Our artist doesn't know much about football! How many mistakes has he made in this picture?

O Tired Dun Fox!

The heading of this page is an anagram of a British football team, that is, a rearrangement of the letters to spell out different words. Can you spot which team it is? And when you've done so, can you work out what all the teams below are? (NB They're all British.)

1   TRACY SCALP ALE.

2   I.E. ONE MUST RUSH.

3   FED, SHE SAID, DENY FLEW.

4   BAN HIM, GRIM.

5   QUEUE, THEN HOOF ST.

6   DIG ELM SHRUB, DO.

7   FROM HOT SENT GIANT.

8   TUM SHOP ROT.

9   TRY ICY OVEN, T.C.

10   MULE INN, FRED.

11   TRAM HERO, H.

12   FRIED ETCH, LES.

54

True or False? I

Are the following statements true or false?

1 You cannot score a goal from a direct free kick.

2 The referee's signal for an indirect free kick is to hold his left arm up in the air.

3 Aluminium studs in football boots are useful on wet, slippery ground.

4 A volley is a pass made by kicking the ball when it's on the ground.

5 You are allowed to stop the ball with your chest provided you don't touch it with your hands or arms.

6 Bobby Moore was a former captain of Scotland.

7 Gary Lineker played for Barcelona.

True or False? II

Are the following statements true or false?

1 Celtic's home ground is Ibrox Park.

2 Ryan Giggs's first international match appearance was for Wales in 1991.

3 Manchester United fans have a song about Ryan Giggs which is sung to the tune of 'Popeye the Sailorman'.

4 Both Andrei Kanchelsis and Eric Cantona play for Tottenham Hotspur.

5 Gheorghe Hagi is Italian.

6 Paul Gascoigne burst into tears at the World Cup semi-final in 1992.

7 You use an overarm throw to throw a ball a long distance and an underarm throw to throw it a short distance.

Spot the Ball

This drawing is based on a real-life photograph, but the ball has been omitted from it. Can you spot where it is?

In the Locker Room

This puzzle is an acrostic. If you solve the clues correctly and fill in the answers in the grid you will find, reading down the arrowed column, something else you might see in the locker room, especially if you're a fan of Chelsea, Sheffield Wednesday or Chesterfield!

1 They're worn on the feet (5)

2 They're used to fasten no.1 (5)

3 Players wear one on their backs (6)

4 A goalkeeper wears one of these (6)

5 You might wear one of these for training (5, 4)

6, 7 You wear these under your socks (4, 4)

8 If there's a shower, you'll need one of these (5)

9 Footwear (5)

10 The top half of your strip (5)

11 The lower half of your strip (6)

12 Goalkeepers wear these (6)

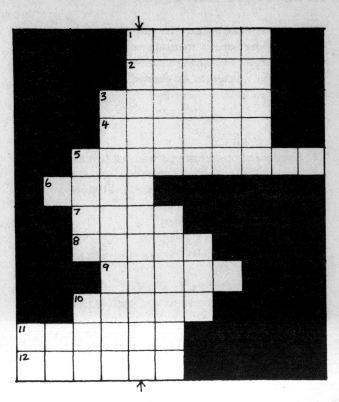

Plus or Minus?

This is a crossword puzzle with a difference. When you have solved the clue, you must either *add* a letter to the word or *subtract* a letter from the word in order to arrive at the answer which must be entered in the grid. The clues tell you which to do.

Across

1 Broad (+ N) (5)
4 Small metal object with pointed end which holds pieces of fabric together, or with which you can fasten a brooch or badge to your clothes (+ S) (4)
6 Fear (– F) (5)
7 A letter might end 'Yours, _ _ _ _' (+ Y) (5)
9 Round marking on a grey horse (– D) (5)
12 Defending player who stays very close to attacking player (– R) (5)
14 The number after six (– S) (4)
15 All the things you need to play football (+ E) (4)
18 Further down (+ S) (6)
20 You _ _ _ _ _ to do this, you should (+ B) (6)
21 Joint at the top of your leg (+ C) (4)

Down

1 There might be one in a playground (– S) (4)
2 It's in the middle of your face (+ I) (5)
3 It might catch a mouse (+ S) (5)
4 Eleven players form one (+ S) (5)
5 This chicken's a great _ _ _ _ _ (+ P) (6)
8 Long for (– E) (4)
10 Creep along quietly in the shadows (– S) (4)
11 Positioned in the middle (– D) (6)
13 Ability (– S) (4)
16 Male deer (– S) (3)
17 The best team is top of the league _ _ _ _ _ (– T) (4)

18 The opposite of 'bottom' (+ S) (4)
19 Alcoholic drink made from grapes (– E) (3)

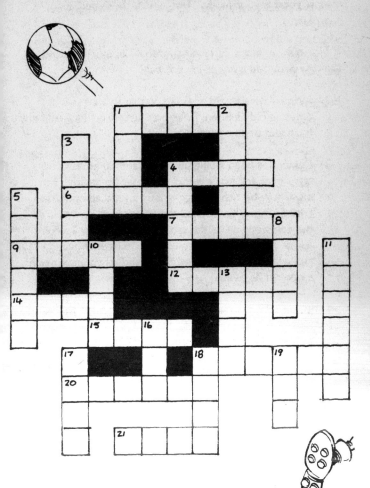

Your Number's Up!

How good is your maths? Test it with these taxing problems.

1   How can a boy carry nine footballs in four bags and have an odd number in each bag?

2   Ryan is twice as old as Brian. When Ryan was four times as old as Brian, Brian was just three. How old are Ryan and Brian?

3   Daniel had been saving up 1p, 2p and 5p coins in his piggy bank for many weeks. One day he decided he must now be rich enough to buy a football book that cost £3.99, so he opened the pigggy bank and poured the coins out on to the table. There were 30 1p coins, 43 2p coins and 17 5p coins. Did he have enough money to buy the football book, and if not, how much more did he need?

4   In the school sports day football tournament there were five teams – A, B, C, D and E. C finished in front of D but behind A. E finished in front of B but behind D. In which order did they finish the tournament?

In the Negative

Which of the pictures below is the one shown in the negative above?

Goal Tally

How many times can you find the word BALL in the grid below; and how many times can you find the word GOAL in the grid opposite? Count carefully – there may be more than you think! The words may read across, up, down or diagonally, either forwards or backwards. They are all in straight lines. Each letter in the grid may be used more than once, but not all of them are necessarily used. Use a pencil and a ruler to cross out the words as you find them.

B	L	A	B	A	L	L	A	B
A	A	B	A	L	L	B	A	A
L	L	L	L	B	L	L	B	L
L	L	L	L	L	L	L	A	L
A	A	A	A	L	L	L	L	A
B	B	B	B	B	A	A	L	B
A	A	A	A	A	B	B	L	A
L	L	L	L	L	L	A	A	L
L	L	L	L	L	A	L	B	L

G	L	O	A	G	O	A	L	A	O	G
O	O	A	L	A	O	G	O	G	O	O
A	A	A	O	G	A	A	O	A	L	A
L	G	G	L	G	L	A	L	A	A	L
A	G	O	A	L	L	G	O	A	L	A
O	A	A	A	G	G	G	O	A	L	O
G	O	L	O	L	O	L	A	A	A	G
O	L	A	O	A	A	A	O	L	O	O
A	L	L	L	O	L	G	L	A	G	A
L	A	A	A	G	O	A	L	O	O	L
O	O	O	O	L	O	A	O	G	A	A
G	G	G	G	O	A	A	G	G	L	O
A	L	A	O	G	O	A	L	A	O	G

Grandstand

How many differences can you spot between these two pictures of a grandstand?

Word Chain

Solve the clues and fill in the letters clockwise in this grid, in which the last letter of one word is the first letter of the one following it.

1 A goalkeeper may bring the ball back into play with this (4)
2 The goal should be your _ _ _ _ _ (6)
3 The team may work these out before a match (7)
4 The goalie's job is to stop people doing this (7)
5 You may be able to slide in one of these near the goal (6, 4)
6 You may use this to bring a dead ball back into play (5-2)
7 The goal is covered by this (7)

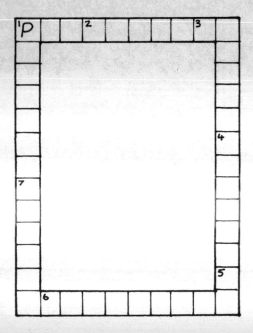

Technical Stuff

1 With what part of your foot do you kick the ball when making a push pass?

2 With which part of your foot do you kick the ball when making a flick pass?

3 What's another name for a banana shot?

4 If you are trying to intercept a ball heading towards you how do you stop it bouncing off your foot?

5 What is 'trapping'?

6 In a side block tackle, do you drag or kick the ball away from your opponent?

7 What are the 'in-swinger' and the 'out-swinger' types of?

8 If you are about to throw in the ball, where do you hold it and throw it from?

9 What does 'screening the ball' mean?

10 What's the point of a chip shot?

Where?

1 Where is the ball placed for the kick-off?

2 If the opposite side is taking a corner kick and the penalty area is crowded, where should the goalkeeper stand?

3 At the kick-off, where should the players be?

4 Where is the Azteca Stadium?

5 Where is the San Paulo Stadium?

6 Where were 95 Liverpool supporters crushed to death and almost 200 injured in 1989?

7 Where can you put an optional flagstaff?

8 Where was the first World Cup Final held in 1930?

9 With which Midlands town was Stanley Matthews associated?

10 Where did the plane carrying Manchester United's team crash in 1958, killing many players?

Team Badges II

Can you identify these European team badges?

1

2

3

4

5

6

Ref's Reference

Could you be a ref? See how much you know about the rules of your favourite game.

1 Can a referee caution a player before the game has started if that player and the referee are on the pitch?

2 What should a referee do if a player appears to be badly hurt?

3 If an incident has occurred in which a free kick would give an advantage to the team in the wrong, what should the referee do?

4 Has the referee the power to prevent people other than the players and linesmen from entering the pitch?

5 What does a referee note on his record card? See how many of the ten things in the answer you can name.

6 What kind of watch should a referee wear?

7 Why are red and yellow cards different shapes?

8 What colour should linesmen's flags be, and who provides them?

9 Can a player be cautioned if he disagrees with the referee's decision?

10 How should the referee hold a red or yellow card?

11 If a player commits a misconduct during the half-time interval, can the referee take action against him?

All Square

Which two squares of this squared-up picture are exactly the same?

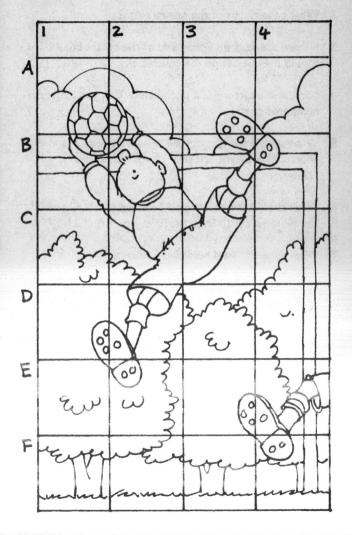

On the Ground

1 What's the minimum width of a soccer pitch?

2 What's the radius of the centre circle?

3 If there are flags on either side of the centre line, should they be set on the touchline?

4 Look at the picture of a pitch below. Can you name the numbered parts?

5 What should the distance be between points A and B? Should it be 22 yds (20.1m), 25 yds (22.8m) or 30 yds (27.4m)?

6 What should the distance be between points C and D? Should it be 2 ft (0.6m), 3 ft (0.9m) or 4 ft (1.21m)?

7 What's the 'six-yard box' also known as?

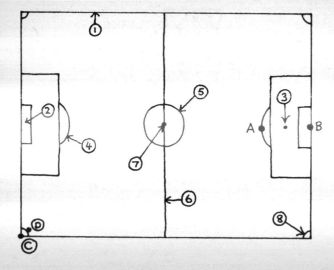

Cup Final Grid

Hidden in each of these grids are two names connected with the 1997 FA Cup Final. Can you spot what they are?

	A	E
E	L	S
H	I	L
C	T	L
U	U	U
R	D	G

B	O	R	N
S	O	Y	A
M	N	R	B
I	S	B	H
D	E	R	G
D	L	O	U

Great Save!

Which of these pictures is the odd one out, and why?

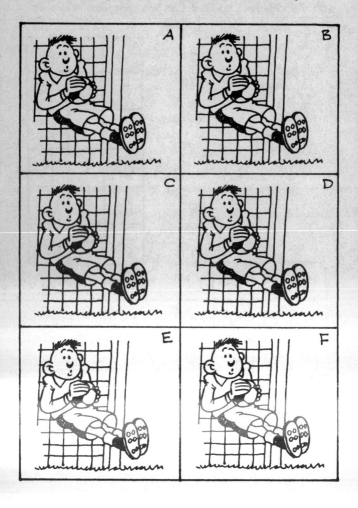

Baffling Brainteasers

1 What's the next number in the series?

11 1 12 1 1 1 2 1 3 1

2 John and Jim are, respectively, Sheffield United and Sheffield Wednesday supporters. One Saturday John's father is taking him to an away match in Manchester, while Jim's dad is taking Jim to an away match in Birmingham. If John and his dad must travel 38 miles to Manchester, and they drive at 40 mph, and Jim and his dad must travel 76 miles to Birmingham and they drive at 50 mph, who gets there first if they both leave at 11 am?

3 If you go to bed at 7.30 on the night the clocks are put forward for British Summer Time, having set your alarm clock to wake you up at 8.30 for football practice the next morning, how much sleep will you get?

4 You want to buy some new football boots and your mum and dad say you must save up for them. If you save 1p the first day, 2p the second day, 4p the third day, 8p the fourth, and so on, saving twice as much each day as you saved the day before, how long will it take you to save enough for the boots if they cost £20?

Missing Lines

Some of the straight lines have disappeared, but can you read the message?

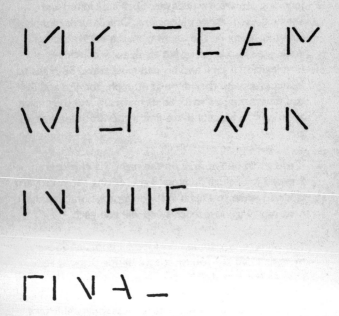

MY TEAM

WILL WIN

IN THE

FINAL

Answers

Page 1 Rules of the Game

1 Eleven. **2** The goalkeeper. **3** Players other than the goalkeeper may move the ball with any part of their body except the hands or arms. **4** Two. **5** With flags. **6** No more than two. **7** 45 minutes. **8** Not more than 15 minutes. **9** The whole of the ball must cross the goal line under the crossbar and between the posts. **10** No. It must cross the touchline completely to be out of play. **11** One from which a goal cannot be scored until the ball has been touched by another player. **12** At least 10 yds (9.14 m) away. **13** At the start of the game it should weigh 14-16 oz (397-454 g). **14** Clothes that are a different colour from those worn by the rest of the players and the referee. **15** Only with the referee's permission.

Page 2 Afternoon Out

1 45 sweets. **2** 32,500. **3** £1.15.

Page 3 Woolly Mufflers

There are 19 football scarves in the picture.

Page 4 Picture Puzzle

Page 6 First Half

There are 10 differences between the pictures.

Page 8 Name-dropping

1 Vinnie Jones. 2 Marco Tardelli. 3 Jurgen Klinsmann.
4 Bobby Charlton. 5 Jean-Pierre Papin. 6 Diego
Maradona. 7 Paul Gascoigne. 8 Kenny Dalglish.
9 Johan Cruyff. 10 Roberto Baggio.
11 Eric Cantona. 12 Gary Lineker.

Page 9 Cup Tie

Picture letter D.

Page 10 Free Kick

The left-over letters spell out FIRST DIVISION.

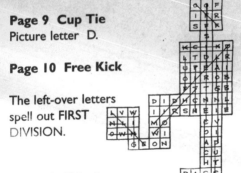

Page 12 Who?

1 Kenny Dalglish. 2 Pele. 3 Eusebio. 4 Diego
Maradona. 5 Johan Cruyff. 6 Billy Wright. 7 Bobby
Moore. 8 Alf Ramsey. 9 Bruce Grobbelaar.
10 Roberto di Matteo

Page 13 On the Line

1 Goal kick. 2 Advise awarding penalty kick.
3 Substitution. 4 Corner kick.

Page 14 Odd One Out
1 Bramall Lane: it is in Sheffield; the other two are in Glasgow.   2 Trapping: it is the art of bringing high or bouncing balls under control; the other two are types of tackle.   3 Juventus: it is an Italian team; the others are Russian.   4 Nacional: it is a team from Uruguay; the others are Brazilian.   5 Link-man: he is a midfield player; the others are forwards.   6 Dribble: it is moving the ball along; the others are shots.   7 Out-swinger: it is a corner kick; the others are goalkeeper's throws.
8 Heading: the others are fouls.   9 Forward short leg: it is a cricket position; the others are football positions.
10 Rose Bowl: it is an American football trophy; the others are soccer trophies.

Page 15 Knotty Problem
Laces A belong to boot 2 ; laces B to boot 3 ; laces C to boot 1.

Page 16 What's in a Name?
1 When the attacker has fewer than two opposing players between him and the goal at the time the ball was played.
2 A kick given as compensation for a foul. It may be direct or indirect.   3 One of a number of offences committed intentionally by a player on his opponent while the ball is in play, such as kicking him, tripping him up, charging at him, holding him, pushing him, and so on.
4 A kick awarded in the penalty area to the attacking side if the defending side have committed one of nine penal offences.   5 If the ball crosses completely over the touchline, this is awarded by the referee to the opposite team and the player who last played it.   6 A card the referee holds up when cautioning a player.   7 A card the referee holds up when sending off a player.   8 Flicking the ball forwards or sideways with the outside of the foot.
9 Cutting the foot across the inside or outside of the ball

to make it 'bend'. **10** Kicking the ball immediately after it bounces. **11** Saving the ball by flinging yourself towards it and ending up on the ground. **12** Deflecting the ball from entering the goal by hitting it with clenched fists.

Page 17 What's Missing?
A Stripe on sleeve. **B** Lock. **C** Peg
D Contents of bag. **E** Laces.

Page 18 Gridlock
I1. 3D. 5G. 7A. 9C. 11G. 13B. 15G.

Page 20 Getting Fit
The arrowed column spells out RYAN GIGGS.

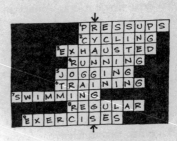

Page 22 Field of Play
1 Outside left. **2** and **3** Centre forwards (strikers).
4 Outside right. **5** and **6** Link-men. **7** Left back.
8 and **9** Centre halves. **10** Right back.
11 Goalkeeper.

Page 23 Fill the Gaps
1 Leeds United. **2** Wimbledon. **3** Charlton Athletic.
4 Chelsea. **5** Manchester United.
6 Tottenham Hotspur. **7** Aston Villa. **8** Bristol Rovers. **9** Preston North End. **10** Partick Thistle.
11 Derby County. **12** Wolverhampton Wanderers.

Page 24 Odd Picture Out
Picture C is the odd one out because grandstand roof is lower.

Page 26 Make It Fit

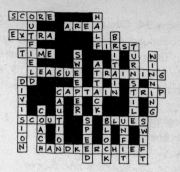

Page 28 Nicknames

1 York City. 2 Sheffield United. 3 Aston Villa.
4 West Ham United. 5 Chelsea. 6 Stoke City.
7 Arsenal. 8 Swansea City. 9 Derby County.
10 Scunthorpe United. 11 Reading. 12 Celtic.
13 Dundee United. 14 Millwall. 15 Mansfield Town.

Page 29 How Many?

There are 8 patterns on the footballs.

Page 30 Word Snake

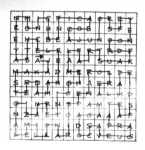

Page 32 Hidden in a Sentence

1 Captain. 2 Defence. 3 Forward. 4 Field.
5 Pitch. 6 Offside. 7 Save. 8 Ball. 9 Team.
10 Corner.

Page 33 Striking

Striker C.

Page 34 Observation Test

1 The player at the bottom right is doing the press-ups.
2 The curly-haired player is lifting weights.   3 Player number 5.   4 Four players.   5 Black shorts and striped shirts.   6 A tracksuit with stripes down the sides of the legs.   7 His left hand.   8 There are 3 trees in the background.   9 Three cows.   10 Two.   11 Player number 7.

Page 36 Results and Records

1 Norman Whiteside.   2 Roberto Baggio.
3 Three, by Geoffrey Charles Hurst, in the England v. West Germany match on 30 July 1966.   4 Manchester United – nine times.   5 £15 million, paid by Newcastle United for Alan Shearer in July 1996 when he transferred from Blackburn Rovers.   6 Peter Shilton – 125 between 1970 and 1990.   7 16, scored by Stephan Stanis in December 1942.   8 Ian Rush of Liverpool in 1983-4.
9 Rangers – 19 times between 1947 and 1993.
10 Liverpool – in 1981-4 and 1995, and Aston Villa in 1961, 1975, 1977, 1994 and 1996.   11 Bobby Charlton, from April 1958 to May 1970.

Page 37 Header!

There are 9 differences.

Page 38 Buying Kit

Buy a shirt, shorts and socks (£53.97); then either boots (b) and football (a) (£87.95); or boots (a) and football (c) (£89.95).

Page 39 Rhyme Time

BOUGHT and court (tennis court); PITCH and witch; CATCH and patch (on trousers); NOTCH and watch; BRISTLE and whistle; GATE and plate; SOCKS and box.

Page 40 Own Goal!

Pictures B and C are exactly the same.

Page 42 Home Grounds

1 Old Trafford. 2 Delle Alpi. 3 Highbury. 4 Non Camp. 5 Vélodrome. 6 Anfield Road. 7 Ibrox Park. 8 Goodison Park. 9 Molineux. 10 Annfield Park. 11 Stamford Bridge. 12 Highfield Road. 13 St Andrews. 14 Loftus Road. 15 Hillsborough.

Page 43 Cup Fever

1 European Cup. 2 World Cup. 3 European Championship Trophy. 4 European Cup-winners' Cup.

Page 44 Pitching In

1 20 yds (18.3 m). 2 5 ft (1.52 m) 3 8 ft (2.44 m) high by 24 ft (7.32 m) wide. 4 Either. 5 The penalty area. 6 No, it must be between 100 and 130 yds long (91-119 m).

Page 45 Team Badges 1

1 Everton. 2 Arsenal. 3 Chelsea. 4 Nottingham Forest. 5 Raith Rovers. 6 Leicester City.

Page 46 Cryptic Crossword

Page 48 Riddle-me-ree

L - I - V - E - R - P - O - O - L.

Page 49 Right and Left

There are 21 right and 15 left boots in the picture.

Page 50
Great Names

Page 52 What's Wrong?

The following things are wrong: goaly wearing same clothes
as other players, player holding ball, two balls in play, rugby
posts, goal netting wrong, sleeping player, dog on pitch,
incorrect markings on pitch.

Page 54 O Tired Dun Fox!*

1 Crystal Palace. 2 Stenhousemuir. 3 Sheffield
Wednesday. 4 Birmingham. 5 Queen of the South.
6 Middlesbrough. 7 Nottingham Forest.
8 Portsmouth. 9 Coventry City. 10 Dunfermline.
11 Rotherham. 12 Chesterfield.

* The heading is an anagram of Oxford United.

Page 55 True or False? I

1 False; you can. 2 True. 3 True. 4 False; it's a
pass made by kicking it when it is in the air. 5 True.
6 False; he was a former captain of England. 7 True.

Page 56 True or False? II

1 False; Ibrox Park is Rangers' home ground. 2 True.
3 False; their song is sung to the tune of 'Robin Hood'.

4 False; though they did both play for Manchester United.
5 False; he is Romanian. **6** False; it was in 1990. **7** True.

**Page 57
Spot the Ball**

Page 58 In the Locker Room

The arrowed column spells out BLUE AND WHITE.

**Page 60
Plus or Minus?**

Page 62 Your Number's Up!

1 He puts three footballs in each of three bags and then puts the three bags into a fourth, larger, bag. **2** Ryan is 18 and Brian is nine. **3** He had saved £2.01 so he still needed another £1.98 to buy the book. **4** A was first, followed by C, D, E and B.

Page 63 In the Negative

Footballer A.

Page 64 Goal Tally

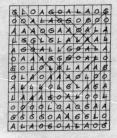

The word BALL appears in the smaller grid 34 times; the word GOAL in the larger grid 42 times.

Page 66 Grandstand

There are 10 differences.

Page 68 Word Chain

```
P U N T A R G E T A
G                 C
N                 T
I                 I
T                 C
T                'S
E                 C
N                 O
I                 R
W                 I
O                 N
R                'G
H T O H S D N U O R
```

Page 69 Technical Stuff

1 The inside.   2 The outside.   3 'Bending' the ball.
4 By keeping your foot as relaxed as possible.   5 The art
of bringing high or bouncing balls under control instantly.
6 Drag it.   7 Corner kick.   8 Behind and over your
head.   9 Shielding it from an opponent with your body.
10 To lift the ball over a short distance.

Page 70 Where?

1 On the centre spot in the middle of the centre circle.
2 Near the centre of the goal.   3 Every player should be
in his own half.   4 Mexico City.   5 Naples.
6 Hillsborough.   7 At either end of the halfway line.
8 Centenario Stadium, Montevideo, Uruguay.
9 Stoke-on-Trent.   10 Munich.

Page 71 Team Badges II

1 Moscow Dynamo.   2 Milan.   3 Go Ahead Eagles
(Holland).   4 FC Bayern München.   5 Valencia.
6 Lille OSC (France).

Page 72 Ref's Reference

1 Yes.   2 Stop the game.   3 Not allow the free kick.
4 Yes.   5 The date, team names and colours, the
captains' numbers, the kick-off times, the score, details of
cautions and dismissals, substitutes, and the linesmen's
names.   6 A stopwatch.   7 So the referee can tell

which is which when the cards are still in his pocket to avoid pulling out the wrong one by mistake. **8** Bright colours. They are provided by the home team. **9** Yes. **10** High up in the air with his arm held vertically. **11** Yes.

Page 73 All Square
Squares D1 and E3 are identical.

Page 74 On the Ground
1 50 yds (45.7 m). **2** 10 yds (9.1 m). **3** No, they must be set back at least 1 yd (0.9 m) from the touchline. **4** 1) Touch line. 2) Goal area. 3) Penalty mark. 4) Penalty arc. 5) Centre circle. 6) Halfway line. 7) Centre mark. 8) Corner area. **5** 22 yds (20.1 m) **6** 3 ft (0.9 m). **7** The goal area.

Page 75 Cup Final Grid
The hidden names are
RUUD GULLIT, CHELSEA
and BRYAN ROBSON,
MIDDLESBROUGH.

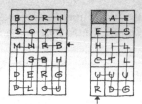

Page 76 Great Save!
Picture D is the odd one out.
Because the goal net is complete beneath his left hand.

Page 77 Baffling Brainteasers
1 4. They are the sequence of chimes of a chiming clock that strikes the hours and half hours, starting with 11 o'clock. **2** John and his dad arrive first at 11.57 am; Jim and his dad arrive at 12.31. **3** One hour. Unless you have a 24-hour clock the alarm will go off at 8.30 pm the same night. **4** Eleven days.

Page 78 Missing Lines
The message reads: MY TEAM WILL WIN IN THE FINAL.